Simpsonly the Best Spiritual Truths

Renea Simpson

Simpsonly the Best Spiritual Truths

ISBN: 978-1-956884-15-9
4th edition
Contributing editors or all services completed
by Imprint Productions Inc.
Cover Design: Ramona C. Parker

Printed in the United State of America
Published by Imprint Productions Inc.
Fourth Edition 2023

Contact
info@imprintproductionsinc.com
\www.imprintproductionsinc.com

A Friend of a Friend

Have you ever had a friend to help you through your troubles? That sits down and prays with you, when you have no other.

Have you ever had a friend that just sat down and cried about all the troubled ways this world is floating by?

Have you ever had a friend that pushes you in the right way each time your struggle brings each and every day.

Have you ever had a friend that holds you at night when the day has been long and no one else is in sight?

Lord. Thank you for being my friend and for knowing exactly what to say. I just look to the hills in prayer. He is there with me, each, and every day.

Content

Open Book

Life is a series of chapters where you fill in the pages, to create a storyline, the storyline playing out until the end being either triumph or tragedy. - Renea Simpson

Naiveness

Childhood to fourteen was priceless; if possible, capture in a bottle to replay over and over, not merely reflect on. Looking through rose-colored glasses I viewed the world as perfect, perfect in the sense of innocence and carefree.

Never had I experienced racism, bigotry, or any ugliness of society.

Knowing about the Civil Right Movement my young mind could not fully grasp the struggles Blacks and other minorities were experiencing.

Like a very protective Mother, Hen Mom sheltered me and my twin sister while our older sibling had 'war stories' to tell yet did not understand it was taboo as long as they lived at home. Mom determined my twin, and I would not hear

of such dark ideas of humanity. determined my twin, and I would not hear of such dark ideas of humanity.

Foolishly in Love

My relationship was like a bad romance Movie where love started good but towards the end failed miserably. Fear of being hurt made me pull away when love got too deep. Twice in my life I gave myself wholly only for love to pull away saying I was too giving, too demanding, too trusting. Over time as I became wiser, I realized I had looked for that fatherly love from guys I dated.

In my book I speak of my mother instilling within me tenacity, perseverance, courage, and patience, all helping me get through being tested and tried by fire, depending on God to see me through it all. The great lesson I learned was, *" Love yourself···the rest will follow and flow."*

Recognition of Praise

Whenever I hear Temptation's hit song, *"Papa Was a Rolling Stone"* I think of my Father. My father was not a good parent, not a good role model, more absent than present in our lives. He was disrespectful, not loving Mom as a man truly loved a woman, so it is no surprise, we do not speak about him, all our conversations are much love praise, adoration to the late great Cora Simpson.

Renee

Throughout history this name has taken a variation but all with one meaning and that meaning is *"rebirth"* But these variants were derived from the first matriarch;" Renata." Renata was the Latin name.

It was used by the Early Roman Christians, taken up temporarily by the 17th century Puritans, and still occasionally used in modern times. In Australia it had the most success, especially popular during the 1970s.

But success gradually faded quietly. The English pronunciation of the name led to variants such as: Rennie, Renie, Renay, Renny, Reney, and Renea.

My name also means "positive thinker." Throughout my life as a character, as one close, another begins, I've kept strong faith in God, optimistic about my future, belief in my writing talent. It is God-given.

–Renea Simpson

Southern Fried...Fire Tried

Hi, I'm Renea. Long story short I am unique positive thinking aquarian love with life born again believe Jesus Christian and I am a die-hard romantic who loves soft music and curling up to a romantic novel my motto is *"love yourself there will follow and flow".*

I remember a popular Coca-Cola commercial that featured my favorite country singer Loretta Lynn. She sang a sixty second piece from her song, "I was Raised on Country Sunshine" (love that song). While the message depicted a cold bottle of Coke quenching one's thirst on a hot summer day, just seeing the image of a Southern living a simple joyful country life made me more appreciative of being born and raised in a small town.

In every sense of the acronym, I am a G.R.I.T.S (Girls raised in the south), and my childhood was priceless. As a matter of fact, childhood innocence was just that. "Innocent." Even though my community was poor economically, we were rich in friend and family togetherness, love, and respect. "Love thy neighbor" was not "sounding brass, twinkling cymbals "~neighbors truly had lone for one another. Children

respected not just the elders, but children respected their parents.
When a child misbehaved, got into trouble, a parent. could render punishment without going to jail or losing custody. My generation, (babies born in the sixties) are the last of the baby boomers. When we as children played all day outside, in the street, until evening and had fun. During our childhood we played "hide and seek" outside at night. We did so without worries or fear of anything happening to us. Such times are no more because society has become more evil and crazier.

Also, my generation were the first who played video games and the last to record songs off the radio onto a cassette tape. We learned how to program a VCR before anyone else. We are the generation of Tom and Jerry, Looney Toons, Electric Company, Zoom, Sesame Street, and Captain Kangaroo. We traveled in cars without seat belts or air bags, lived without cell phones and caller ID.

Above all else, God was the center of our lives, Matthew 6:33 was very necessary before starting your day. I remember my third-grade teacher, Mrs. Walton, having morning prayer each morning before class. Even though there were a few unruly students, the power of prayer given by old

schoolteachers made the learning and school days go by smoothly and exciting.
Even though those nostalgic days are gone, I recall how we all had a great time. The priceless things advancement in science and technology can never ever replace are the seven fruits of the spirit (Galatians 5:22, 33), people in my community practiced in action, not merely words.

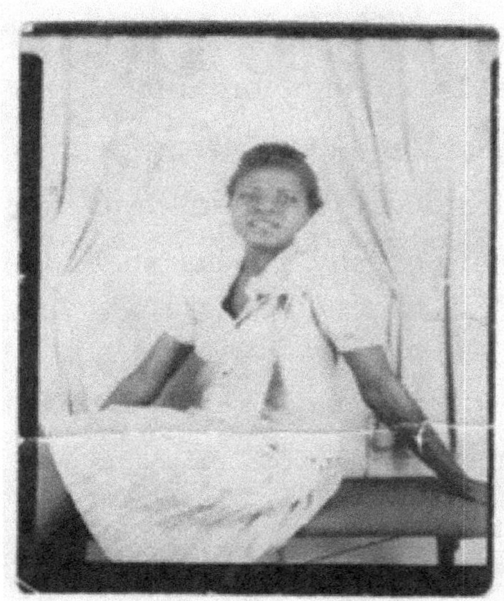

Cora Elizabeth Reeder

Lighthouse in the Midst of the Storm

My mother was the epitome of a virtuous woman... a strong Black woman possessing a "strong constitution" she often said. In my eyes she was a woman of resilience, courage. She was virtuous, loving and had an undying spirit and faith in God. Just like a Lighthouse being battered by an angry sea and withstanding the turbulent winds and rain my mother, by God's grace, protection, she over, withstood every obstacle, every persecution coming against her. Her life, she described, as that of a job's life and she often quoted Job 13:15,16. "Though he slays me, yet will I trust in Him: but I

will maintain my own ways before him. He also shall be my salvation: for a hypocrite shall not come before him."

Through her 88 years of life, she talked of no regrets, knowing through it all she learned to trust in Jesus, she learned to trust in God. I can honestly say her shoes are much too big for me to fill.

Cora Reeder's daughter

My mother instilled within me tenacity. perseverance, courage and patience. In my own life these helped me get through being tested and tried by fire, depending on God to see me through it all.

"Wear the world as a loose garment" she often told me. As I grew older, I realized what those words meant.

What is Passion but love whatever one does in life... an avoid interest as in a hobby; a driving attraction to something which grows out of motivation or attitude. I discovered my gift, my passion for writing at age twelve.

English has always been my favorite subject (along with science and history), from grade school through high school I excelled with A's and B's grades. In 9th grade I presented my first short story writing, the grade I received being A+. It was an "ah ha" moment for me as well as my teacher, Mrs. Nash.

Recently I decided to write professionally, presenting my gift to the world. Proverbs 17:8 states, “A gift is as precious stone in the eyes of him that hath it: whithersoever it turneth, it is prospereth.” I present my gift to you. It is my prayer that each word touches someone’s heart.

I am constantly visioning...

Stay tuned!

My Moto:

Love yourself...

The rest will follow and flow!

Renea Simpson

Stand The Storm

Stand the Storm it won’t be long.
“Tll you woke up By and by Tho’ rain must fall
In your life Troubles, heartaches.
Oh, so much strife.
Puts your back up against the wall --
You’ve given it every ounce of your all. Remember...God
has heard your call.
When the wind's force increases strong
Keep vision, keep dreams.
Forever reaching for the sky.

Renea Simpson

Love Under the Rainbow

My face is all aglow each time I look up, see the color of eight shaped bows in the sky above me.
The illustrious Rainbow a covenant established between God and Noah, and onward to all-an everlasting promise from JEHOVAH...a token of HIS love placed in Heavenly skies above! Love under the rainbow created to let us know never again will. HE destroys all flesh upon the earth.
NO... No... No! My marvelous loving God repented, replanted, rebirthed, sent eight. People forth from the Ark to make a fresh start (I.e., new beginning). Noah's sons and their wives soon repopulated the earth after forty days and nights God saved their lives.

Message Behind the Rainbow

If a reminder of the promise (covenant) God established between HIMSELF, Noah and now to every believer that He would no longer destroy HIS creations. By looking "up" when we see the Rainbow, we have hope and faith in God's word... also the promise of salvation. So, the Rainbow is salvation, as well as fruits of the spirit: love, joy, peace, long suffering, gentleness, faith, meekness, and temperance, the actions God did for us. Galatians 5:22-23.

The word Rain is mentioned in Revelation 4: 3. Here it is situated around the throne of God, and to me that is God's way of looking at HIS promise; it symbolizes the ark He chose to use when He made a covenant, first to Noah, eventually to every believer.

In Ezekiel 1:22 "rainbow" represents Heaven's majestic beauty and awesomeness. In Ezekiel 1:28 "rainbow" brightness after a rain, the Light and the Glory of GOD.

Renea Simpson

Who's the Man?

And God said, let there be Light. Genesis 1:3

Once I found my world in darkness until His marvelous light gave me sight. 'Now' I live each day giving Him honor and praise never forgetting to go down on my knees and pray. Have a dialogue with Him because He's my Father above Him there is no other. And, oh yes, I thank Him for Jesus His beloved, begotten son, the *"Bright and Morning Star " Jesus* the Man! Jesus so cool He knows He's "the Man" when He said, "I am the Way, the Truth, and the Life⋯ no man, cometh unto the Father but by Me." Yeah, that's power...

I Love you, Jesus You're the Man!

Renea Simpson

Nurses' Day

NURSES' DAY: May 6th

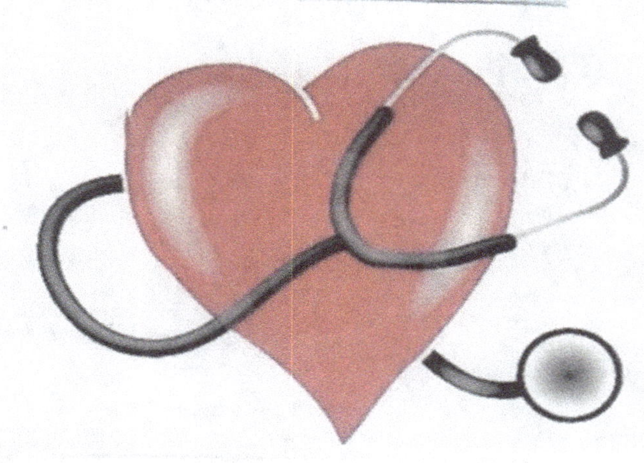

Reasons Why People Select Nursing As a Career

NATIONAL **NURSES DAY**. National **Nurses Day** is observed annually on **May 6**. On this day, we raise awareness of all nurse contributions and commitments and acknowledge the vital role nurses play in society. This day is also the first day of National **Nurses Week** and is sometimes known as National RN Recognition Day.

National **Nurses Day** is celebrated annually on **May 6** to raise awareness of the important role nurses play in society. It marks the beginning of National **Nurses Week**, which ends on May 12, the birthday of Florence Nightingale.

National Nurses Week History

National Nurses Week begins each year on May 6th and ends on May 12th, Florence Nightingale's birthday. These permanent dates enhance planning and position National Nurses Week as an established recognition event. As of 1998, May 8 was designated as **National Student Nurses Day**, to be celebrated annually. And as of 2003, **National School Nurse Day** is celebrated on the Wednesday within National Nurses Week (May 6-12) each year.

The nursing profession has been supported and promoted by the American Nurses Association (ANA) since 1896. Each of ANA's state and territorial nurses associations promotes the nursing profession at the state and regional levels. Each conducts celebrations on these dates to recognize the contributions that nurses and nursing make to the community.

The ANA supports and encourages National Nurses Week recognition programs through the state and district nurses associations, other specialty nursing organizations, educational facilities, and independent health care companies and institutions.

A Brief History of National Nurses Week

1953 Dorothy Sutherland of the U.S. Department of Health, Education, and Welfare sent a proposal to President Eisenhower to proclaim a "Nurse Day" in October of the following year. The proclamation was never made.

1954 National Nurse Week was observed from October 11 - 16. The year of the observance marked the 100th anniversary of Florence Nightingale's mission to Crimea. Representative Frances P. Bolton sponsored the bill for a nurse week. Apparently, a bill for a National Nurse Week was introduced in the 1955 Congress, but no action was taken. Congress discontinued its practice of joint resolutions for national weeks of various kinds.

1972 Again a resolution was presented by the House of Representatives for the President to proclaim "National Registered Nurse Day." It did not occur.

1974 In January of that year, the International Council of Nurses (ICN) proclaimed that May 12 would be "International Nurse Day." (May 12 is the birthday of Florence Nightingale.) Since 1965, the ICN has celebrated "International Nurse Day."

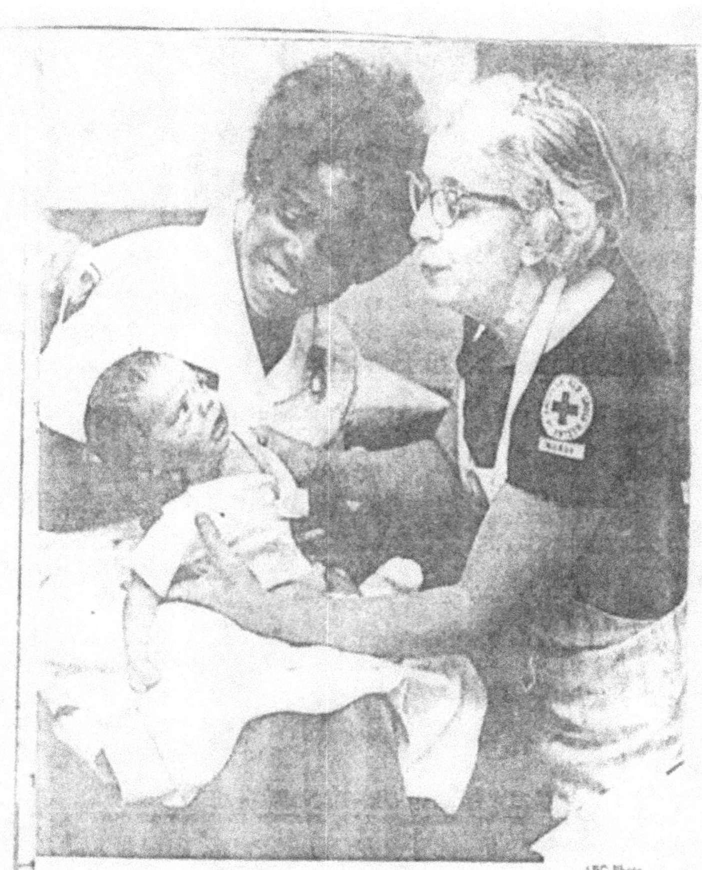

ARC Photo

Tony Lee Glass, son of Mr. and Mrs. Jay A. Glass, at four weeks of age, was believed to be the youngest of 550 returnees from the Middle East arriving at John F. Kennedy International Airport, on Long Island, New York, in June 1967. He was en route with his mother to their home in Nelsonville, Ohio, after leaving Wheelus Air Force Base in Libya. Tony is ministered to by Sp/5 Christine Matthews of EAC Company, Fort Dix, New Jersey, and Mrs. Margaret M. Aldrich, director of Nursing Services, New York Chapter of the American Red Cross. An additional 1,110 returnees also arrived at McGuire AFB in New Jersey over the same weekend.

1974 In February of that year, a week was designated by the White House as National Nurse Week, and President Nixon issued a proclamation.

1978 New Jersey Governor Brendon Byrne declared May 6 as "Nurses Day." Edward Scanlan, of Red Bank, N.J., took up the cause to perpetuate the recognition of nurses in his state. Mr. Scanlan had this date listed in Chase's Calendar of Annual Events. He promoted the celebration on his own.

1981 ANA, along with various nursing organizations, rallied to support a resolution initiated by nurses in New Mexico, through their Congressman, Manuel Lujan, to have May 6, 1982, established as "National Recognition Day for Nurses."

1982 In February, the ANA Board of Directors formally acknowledged May 6, 1982 as "National Nurses Day." The action affirmed a joint resolution of the United States Congress designating May 6 as "National Recognition Day for Nurses."

1982 President Ronald Reagan signed a proclamation on March 25, proclaiming "National Recognition Day for Nurses" to be May 6, 1982.

1990 The ANA Board of Directors expanded the recognition of nurses to a week-long celebration, declaring May 6 - 12, 1991, as National Nurses Week.

1993 The ANA Board of Directors designated May 6 - 12 as permanent dates to observe National Nurses Week in 1994 and in all subsequent years.

1996 The ANA initiated "National RN Recognition Day" on May 6, 1996, to honor the nation's indispensable registered nurses for their tireless commitment 365 days a year. The ANA encourages its state and territorial nurses associations and other organizations to acknowledge May 6, 1996 as "National RN Recognition Day."

1997 The ANA Board of Directors, at the request of the National Student Nurses Association, designated May 8 as National Student Nurses Day.

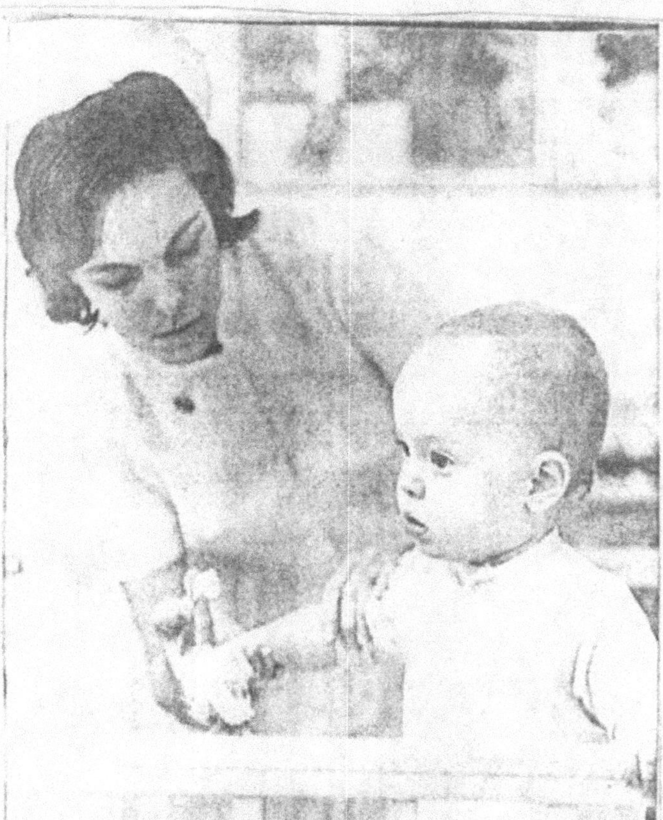

Judith Lewis Photograph

A pediatric nurse treating an apprehensive fourteen-month-old little girl.

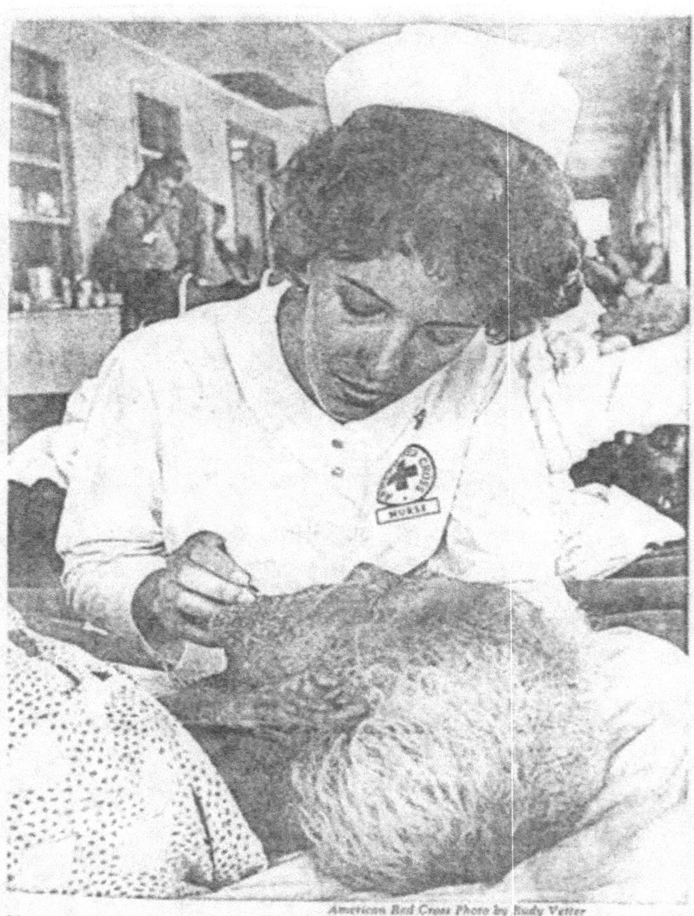

American Red Cross Photo by Rudy Vetter

New Orleans, La., Sept., 1965. A nurse, Merlene Waltman, tends an elderly victim who found safe haven in a Red Cross shelter when Hurricane Betsy battered Louisiana and other Gulf Coast states. Red Cross housed and fed over 200,000 persons, providing nursing and medical care, and helped repair homes – all as an outright gift.

I Surgery

Doctor! Doctor! Another patient has just been brought into the emergency room!! Nurse Grace Ann Mercy hurried into doctor The -Way-The-Truth The-Life Is spacious office, her voice a sense of urgency. The Great Physician was cleaning up from a previous "heart" surgery that called for the great Physician's experienced hands to enter the unconscious patient's chest, removing the old evil, stone-cold, unfeeling-literally "dead" heart, replacing it with a *warm,* good, living-kindness--literally living heart. Looking around at Nurse Grace's frantic face, the Great Physician spoke calmly. *"Do worry··· give me thirty minutes, I will come and perform the surgery and heal the patient."*

Smiling and nodding, relief, Nurse Grace left just as hurriedly out the spacious office, delivering the Good News to the emergency room staff. Taking a seat at his great white desk the Great Physician picked up the black folder and pulled out the new patient's medical history, reading it over. Where his previous patient's diagnosis was "evil-ism" this patient suffered with narcissism, or in street *terms, "I-*ism." Medical history reported that this was an age-old " cancer" that developed around the patient's turning two years of age. The only child of "overly enabling" parents, she was given anything and everything she desired,

absolutely nothing was off limits. Because they spoiled her rotten, she soon developed a "me-myself-and-*I*" attitude, believing everyone should worship the ground she walked upon, literally 'bow down" and serve her at every beck and call. Her attitude got so "stank" she began losing true friends... She went in and out of relationships like a revolving door losing good, marriage minded men. Within a ten-year span she lost both parents, and unfortunately, her dignity. Now at the age of forty she felt hopeless, alone, rejected... The only people who loved and served her are now gone.

Wanting to commit suicide, yet knowing it was an unforgivable sin, she turned to the only other alternative. She made up her mind to seek the Great Physician, have "I " surgery, and be healed of this cancer.

Entering the surgery room, the Great Physician glanced around at His surgical staff. They cleared the path for the Great Physician to walk through; they knew their only function was to watch and observe, be witnesses to the Great Physician do His righteous work on His patient.

The surgical staff looked on as the Great Physician laid hands upon the patient's head. With no use of surgical instruments, the Great Physician's high, above average 20/20 vision, examined his patient's head. The Great Physician's fingers penetrated the patient's skull, lovely meticulously

removing the cancer. The surgical staff clocked the surgery. It took less than five minutes! Once the surgery was done, the surgical staff fell at the Great Physician's feet and gave him praise, honor and glory, for once again He worked a miracle!

After an honor's recovery, the unconscious patient awakes, comes to himself, within that a miracle had taken place-she was cured of "*I*-ism." Sitting up in bed just as the Great physician entered his room, she cried out tears of joy. When he neared her bed, she jumped out of it, fell at his feet, giving him honor and glory!

Moral of the story:

Let not your heart be troubled: ye believe in God, Believe also in me. * In my father's house there are many mansions, if it were not so, I would have told you. And if I go and prepare a place for you, I will come again, and receive you unto myself; that where I am, there ye may be also. And whither I go ye know, and the way ye know. Thomas said unto him, Lord, we know not whither thou goest'; and how can we know the way?

Jesus saith unto him, "*I am the way, the truth, and the life: no man cometh unto the Father, but by me.*"--John 14:1-6

Renea Simpson

01/23/2015

Inner Child

One eternal hour child sat innocently locked into nature. Same time wanting freedom to run through meadows, Spread Wings, fly as far as imagination carried.

"But"

Adult set in···. child was kept hostage to afraid going back to days Life was carefree, full of un-restrictions unbiased opinions laughter, laughter, laughter,

"loving"

being me, mind containing constant possibilities. I kept a child hostage and settled fitting in with the norm Even as the child cried, craved attention, not silence, pleading I partake in innocence if only for an hour... one eternal hour.

Renea Simpson

Eternal hour makes eternity a bit more comprehensive.

That our sons may be as plants grown up in their youth; that our daughters may be as cornerstones, polished after the similitude of a palace. Psalm 144:12

Jesus Explain Greatness

At the same time came the disciples unto Jesus, saying, " *Who is the greatest in the kingdom of heaven?"* And Jesus called a little child unto him, and set him in the midst of them, and said, "Verily I say unto you, except ye be converted, and become as little children, ye shall not enter into the kingdom of heaven.

Whosoever therefore shall humble himself as this little child, the same is greatest in the kingdom of heaven. And who so shall receive one such little child in my name receiveth me."

The Art of Greatness

Greatness: State (position) of having great power, excellence. Being eminent (high exalted, worldly renown); majestic.

Muhammad Ali self-proclaimed, “I am the Greatest” was heard at nearly every interview he gave. Of course, he was saying he is the greatest boxer of all time---had he known he was referencing Almighty God, The Great I AM, WHO gave Ali power to become the greatest boxer in history.

God is possessor of all qualifications of greatness; it would take forever to convey all HIS greatness and still not find enough adjectives. A man after God’s own heart, David gave thanksgiving and prayer; he blessed the Lord. God before all the congregation of Israel:

“Thine, O Lord, is the greatness, and the power, and the glory, and he victory, and the majesty: for all that is the heaven and in the earth is thine: thine is the Kingdom, O Lord, thou art exalted as head overall. Both rich and honor come to thee and thou reignest overall; and in thine hand is power and mighty; and the thine hand it is to make great, and to give strength unto all. 1 Corinthian 29:10-12

Greatness is an art, a practical skill, a profession of a God's

giving gifts 1 Corinthians 12: 1-11 speaks on Spiritual gifts, how great a person becomes by using them to glorify God. Paul has the gift of speaking thirteen different languages so enabling him to spread the gospel throughout the world, to places the disciples could not go.

Jesus made greatness a beautiful work of art through his earthly occupations. As a carpenter he was a professional of building crafts. As a carpenter he laid the corner-stone (stone using the corner of two walls. It is the principal stone) when he built a house. Much later when he began his earthly ministry Jesus took a carpenter to the higher level, a building and a crafting, he disciples so they may become living cornerstones, as Jesus had become.

1 Peter 2:4-8 Jesus made greatness a beautiful work of art through characters, power, and love.

Characters: From the cradle to the grave for three days Jesus remained humble, he carried out God's wishes and redeemed man. John 3: 16

Power: Contrary to the belief of His enemies, Jesus' humbleness did not mean he was weak. In his own words " he said no man has power to take my life. I alone have power to lay it down and raise it up" Jesus has power over His life. Matthew 28:18, John 10:18, John 17:2,

John 19:10-11

Jesus exerted power by cleansing the Temple.

John 2: 16

Jesus resisted Satan's temptations, showing power over the flesh. Matthew 4:11

Jesus gave credit to whom credit is due.

John 13:13-17

Lastly Jesus explained greatness.

Matthew 18:1-5, Mark 9:33-37

Jesus paints a picture of greatness as a person being humble as a child.

Luke 22:24-30

Jesus expounds on who is greasby washing off the disciples' feet.

John 13:5.

Renea Simpson
02/17/2015

Definition of God

Father of the ages
Author and Finisher
Of all things.
Ruler and Judge
O'er man's carnal nature
"past"
"present"
"future"
Millennia.
Such an awesome Being!
Whose greatness
Make the impossible possible!
For time until time eternal God proves.
It is impossible for HIM.
To "lie" or "fail"
Renea Simpson

Life is a Rose

(Spring is Rebirth)

In the springtime when all the things are new, sweet dew " saturates" Earth lifeless vision vegetation and trees undergo newness, shining light pure gold. Life, like a rose, springs forth in a gentle, quiet, and magnificent beauty for all the world to behold it is finished products catching gentle quiet breeze of the wind while slow drops of rain trickling down each rose petal meet the ground un-noise' sound silvery, silvery drop splattering breaking apart like metal after a seismic blast. Such is rain 's duty to die a soft sweet death while replenishing life and give rebirth.

Love: Action, Characteristic, and Power

"In the beginning "three.... words (Genesis 1:1 and John 1:1) conveying an absolute, a bold statement, an announcement of a wonderful event about to unfold.

What is a wonderful event? To answer this question, consider the Bible a great spirit Shakespeare play. Two elements involved is theme and plot 1 John 4:8 tells us *"He that loveth not knoweth not God; for God is love" Here's the theme is "love."* And the source from where love flows is God so God becomes the action of love.

Next comes the plot (plan). Genesis 3:15 shows us that Satan 's plot failed when God stepped in and put his own plan into action. "And I will put enmity between thee and the women, and between thy seed and her seed; it shall bruise thy head, and thou shall bruise his heel." Here the plot is "put enmity " Certainly God "all knowing" knew Satan would plant his bad seed (sin) so God devised a way for man to be saved. John 3:16 says, *"For God so love the world he gave his only begotten son, that whosoever believeth in him shall not perish but have everlasting life."* Here the action he "love" and "gave." Again, God acted on love when He unconditionally sent Jesus into the world to redeem man.

So-what are love characteristics? 1Corinthians 13:4-8, Romans 13:10, Proverbs 10:10 speak on love's character. '

Suffering long" .... certainly, God did So with great patience and surely Christ did so by giving through persecution and death on a Romans cross "worketh it no evil" nor "fulfill the laws" ...truly Jesus did no evil to his enemy and his death completed the laws of Moses 3 great statements given of working no evil be love and found in Matthews 5:11 and 12:45-44 and Luke 6:22.

Last, there is the power of love. 1 Corinthians 13:13 tells us how love is the greatest of faith and hope. 2 Timothy 1:7 let us know God gave the power of love, not fear. 1 John 4-18 tells how perfect love casteth out fears and Proverbs 10:12 makes love's power complete by standing how it covers all sins.

Renea Simpson
02/14/2014

The Way of Love

Love adds a precious seeing to the eyes; a lover's eyes will glaze an eagle blind. And leads me to your eyes, where I o'erlook. Love stories written in love's richest book. Shakespeare says it best~

The Way of Love Me

Woke me up this morning to a beautiful Sunny day
Starting with conversations to my Heavenly Father
"thanking Him", for blessings, to witness another day.
Coffee, a bite of breakfast "whilst" singing, humming
immense happiness along the way!
This is the way God loves me when I give him praise! This is the way God loves me when I acknowledge Jesus when I call on his divine holy name!

Renea Simpson
01/17/2014

Seeking Is Motivation Based on F.A.I.T.H

By Renea Simpson

Hebrews 11:1 state, *"Now faith is the substance of things hoped for, the evidence of things not seen."* I define the acronym of faith as, *"Forward Advancement in True Holiness."*

Forward: not looking back, straight ahead as you are seeking for, seeking after, someone or something.

*Andrew sought after Jesus once he (Andrew) listened intently to John the Baptist preach on the Coming Messiah Upon finding Jesus Andrew asked him, "Rabbi, where dwellest thou?" Jesus simply replied, "Come and see." (John 1:19-40).

*The ten lepers sought Jesus to heal their leprosy. (Luke 17:11-19).

*The woman with the issue of blood sought Jesus to heal her infirmity (Matthew 9:20).

*The widow who lost her coin sought for it diligently until she found it...an example of steadfast perseverance for Jesus.

*Pharisees sought after Jesus for interior motives, to entrap him.

*Paul looked ahead, doing his work for Christ (Philippians 3:13-14) Advancement: moving forward from where you were previously.
*David advanced from a shepherd boy to king of Israel... anointed by Samuel, appointed by God (Exodus 3:1-22).
*Joseph advanced from a slave to overseer of Potiphar's house, and again going through personal tragedies, he advanced from prisoner in an Egyptian prison to Governor over Egypt (Genesis 41:14-53).
*Paul advances as he continues doing his work for Christ (Philippians 3:1314).
*The twelve disciples went from being simple fishermen to "fishers of men" Jesus giving them the Great Commission to spread the Gospel to the world. (Mark 1:17, 16:14-18).

In: preposition meaning *"within the confines of; inside."* It denotes position, location, or condition. Indicates not lacking or without. In, into, within or inward.
Jesus knows what is inside the heart, the mindset of man:
*But Jesus did not commit himself unto them, because he knew all men. And needed not that any should testify of man: For he knew what is inside the heart, the mindset of man. (John 2:24, 25).
*To die in Christ is gain (Philippians 1:21). *Christ lives inside a believer (Genesis 2:20).

*Living in the Holy Spirit (Romans 8-9-10).

True: adjective. Consistent with fact and reality. Not false or erroneous. Real, genuine, faithful, friend, steadfast, loyal, honorable. Upright on unfeigned not fake. Unswervingly, rightly, truthfully.

*Jesus declared himself the highway to heaven (John 14:6).

*Jesus, the true vine (John 15:1).

*Walking in true holiness (Ephesians 4:24).

Holiness: noun. The state of quality of being holy (associated with divine power living according to the religion or spiritual system).

*Glorious this in holiness (Ephesians 15:11).

*Way of holiness (Isaiah 35:8).

*Perfecting holiness (2 Corinthians 7:1)

Renea Simpson

8/7/14

Un Rapped

"Listen."
There was a time I loved the rhythm, the rhyme… blessed it, what is the best music yet!
"On drop of a dime"
In went a CD or a cassette, beat at once popping,
my body "b-bopping" fingers snapping while my favorite artist began rapping.
"I"
Staying awake late would not hesitate.
getting cheap thrills off an artist's
"Killer skills."
"Now"
I've moved on that's all gone,
"don't"
get me wrong that had, with me,

romantic space,
"today"

I'm at a different time, different place
"I'm"
Dancing, singing, humming
to music uplifting,
"strumming"
Holy spirit giving!
"taking"
me higher as I give my all to
"The Man"
I call My Lord and Savior,
I give worship and praise to
"The Man"
Who inspires me to be better, to become free?
"cause"
He sees potential in me!
"yes"
his love sets my soul on fire
moves me higher and higher!
"no no no"
I would never go back nor grow slack,
"Sorry to say"
"today"

most of that stuff is whack!
"anyway"
I'm glad I un-snapped
"happy to proclaim"
I'm un-rapped.

Renea Simpson
12-12-14

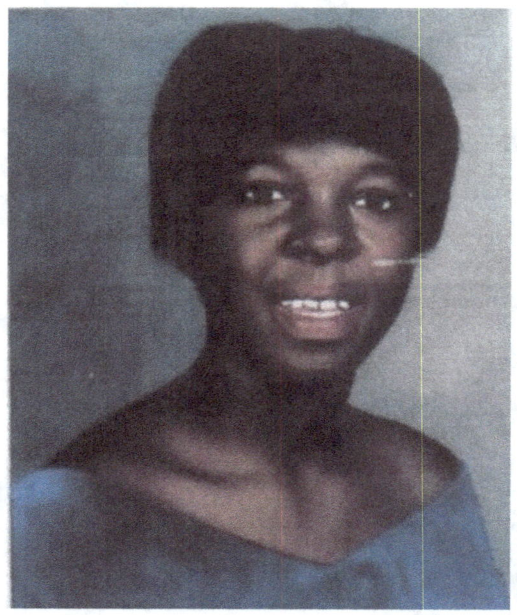

Mattie Lou Simpson

Angel Dwell Amongst Love's Eternal Flames

Like a sweet song she lived amongst everyone's so beautiful so happy a smile always upon her angelic face. Like us all she endured trials and tribulations "Yet" she rode out her storms with patience and grace, her interest strength given by God's great grace.

~Renea Simpson

Godly Mother

A Godly Mother is epitome of a virtuous woman

January 15, 2014 at 2:06pm

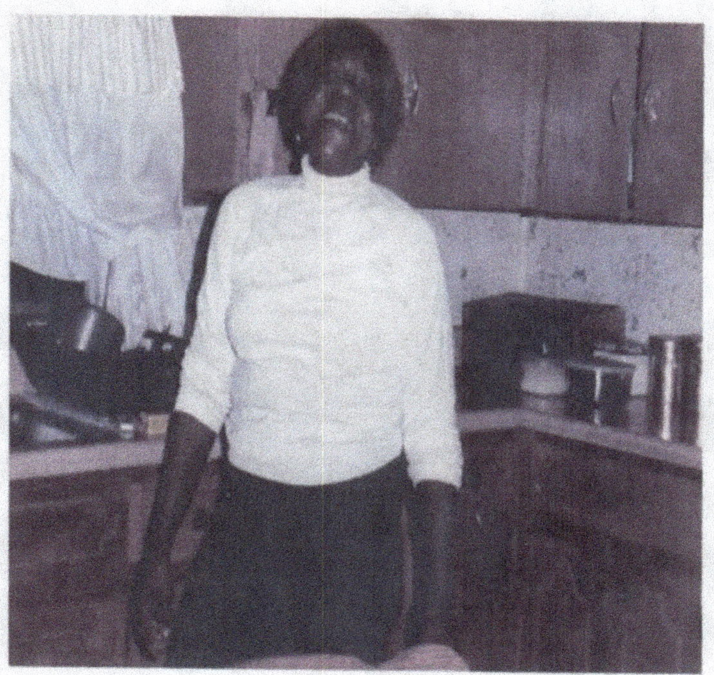

Cora Elizabeth...born during *"The Roaring Twenties"*
Alumna of the greatest generation ever lived.

As a child
I recall
Her rising early each morning
preparing herself for the day...
a song in her heart,
escaping her lips,
filling the house
"with love"
letting Jesus' Holy Spirit
guide her along the way
"then"
waking me, and my siblings

after having prepared breakfast...

Most of those mornings
"We" acted a hot mess
"still"
she somehow made order
out of chaos and confusion
"yes"
Mom was the best!
classic Master Sargeant
holding down the fort,
laying down her rules
before sending us off to school.

Mom's life lessons were words of wisdom,
"We" let sink deep in our hearts, our souls,
even if and when we went astray
and did wrong.

When she scolded and reprimanded,
her tongue was not scathing nor bitter,
only of tough love and kindness
"This will hurt me more than it will hurt you."
she often would say...
on many a day
I was young, dumb, often disobeyed
"now older, wiser"
I realize what her words conveyed.

Cora Elizabeth...a Godly mother...epitome of a virtuous woman
"Her"
BELIEF was God can do anything but fail
FAITH was relying totally on Him
STRENGTH was prayer and perseverance
DRIVING FORCE was the Holy Spirit and endurance
ROCK was Co-Pilot Jesus
LIFE was Pilot Almighty God

"Almighty God, I want you to hold me in the hollow of Your hands."

Renea Simpson
1/15/2014

ref: Proverbs 31

God and Momma

In the midst of my dilemma, I cry out, most times to God...other times to Momma. Both know me "better" than I know myself.

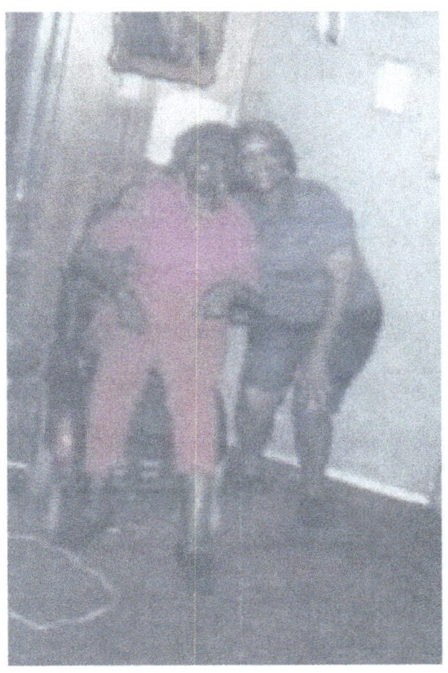

"So" writing this personal letter each is watching over me, giving courage, when none is left... "that" positivity sets my spirit free, Sons acquire independence young... fly out of the proverbial nest early. "But" a daughter remains a child slow to leave home, "grounded" not running wild even at an accountable age, Independence advances life's next stage.

God

And

Momma...

Momma

And

God...

Thank Heaven for their presence! Because, in them, was/is life... in them, love is King, truly wonderful, blessed, beautiful thing! Ingredients “salting” The Earth with powerful eternal essence.

Renea Simpson

Love Letter to Mom

Sweetest, most kind woman I've known never, ever, forgotten even though she's gone "still" I'm learning to make it on my own.

Standing outside, in the big backyard, remembering when she and daddy raised a garden every year "I" looked up towards Heaven in my eye a shed tear, recalling her encouraging words to me, *"Renea follow your dreams you can be anything you want to be!"* This year I strive to move forward, forgetting mistakes that could pull me backward. " So" Mom, I say to you, as I have so many times you were " physically" alive, "I love you!" "always" So blessed God made you mine.

Love,

Renea Simpson

12.13.14

Women of God's House

(We will not forsake Gods house)

We're average, from all walks of life on a mission, doing God's will to touch, save a last life while "keeping it real" that is our motivation.

Our foremost attitude is allowing God to strengthen our fortitude. We remain ladies, according to the Covent:

Galatians 5:22, 23

"Fruit of the Spirit is our theme."

Deuteronomy 8:12

"We believe in a good foundation."

Kings 20:1

"We keep order." P

Psalm 28:8

"No evil will live therein.

Proverbs 12:7

“Only Godly people are allowed to stay.”

Ecclesiastes 12: 3

“We will be good stewards.”

Isaiah 64:11

“God’s house will be eye candy to those wanting redemption.”

Mark 3:25

“No such animal will enter in”

Proverbs 31: 27, 12:4 31:10.

“Examples we follow.”

Renea Simpson

Prayer of Relief

Today, tears of joy did I cry.
When at the mailbox I pulled out
A Letter from my guy.
"God"
Thanks for listening as I pray...
 with your marvelous power you
 caused my sweet man to send a
 letter my way.
I thought he was upset with me,
I thought he no longer loved me
"but" reading his sweet letter
I should have known better
"nothing"
Could never ever forever
change our love for each other!

Renea Simpson

Single Ready to Mingle

"But seek ye first the kingdom of God, and HIS righteousness, and all these things shall be added unto you. " Matthew 6:33

"Looking for love in all the wrong places."
A popular song back in the eighties and still holds true today. It is amazing how people fall for "the banana-in-the-tailpipe" so to speak, especially when I come to "reality" shows like The Bachelor. Seems like such shows, not to mention social media outlets designed to hook a person to find that perfect match, that true love, are all about "m-o-n-e-y."
When you seek God's help finding love HE never fails you. To receive HIS help, you must be totally into him and Jesus Christ. "Falling in love with Jesus' ' as the long implies.

Abraham sought God' face when he searched for a wife for Isaac. He sent his oldest servant to find a wife for Isaac. That servant did not depend upon his morals, he prayed to God to send forth the women who would eventually become Isaac's wife. God answered the servant's prayer by sending Rebekah to the well.

Your "well" could be whatever place God directs you to go and wait upon His answer. HE does everything in order, the outcome is always positive. Lean upon HIM and not to your own understanding and HE will direct your path.

Renea Simpson

Celestial Courtship

Night the moon kissed the earth was a
Heavenly mirth!
The moon, unusually
"large"
"ominous"
"bright"
Was a "fright" And "majestic sight!"
Stars, and all earthly beings, humans like me,
gave witness we could plainly see silver moon
reach out,
"kiss" Earth tenderly upon her mouth.
Renea Simpson
June 22, 2013

A Conversation with God

Dear Heavenly Father,

Full of mercy, grace Please hear me! While I lay prostrate on my face. I remember you told me, "Call upon Me, when you are in trouble, when you need Me... I will answer." "So" I'm calling upon You, right now, I face a dilemma. Too "big" Too "difficult" for me. I've "secretly" Conveyed it all to You. "Thanks, in advance"
For deliverance, for making your words so true.
Renea Simpson
12.13.14

A Break of Day

"I'm" meeting mornings with a smile, appreciating God giving life, as a mother gives birth to her child.
Never dwell on past mistakes, "seize hold' opportunities while it's not too late!
"Tomorrows make futures."
Only God knows one's fate. Realize life is not a "game..."
Once fortune and fame" evaporate" "fade to black" "corrode " "die" all gone in the twinkling of an eye, memories are all that's left, "go" pray you have left "a good name."
Monies are really "accumulated blessings" from God's banks.
Timely deposits to reap an abundant withdrawal.

Renea Simpson
12.13.14

God Has Got Your Back

When life is out of sync a total mess- completely whack! " Don't despair" do not allow doubt, cause you to think, "God doesn't want to remove, from me, the bitter cup I drink." " No! No! No! God is never slack concerning His Promise! Never behooves you to become a "doubting Thomas" God is not a man He should lie, no respecter of persons, "black" "brown" "yellow" "red" "white" God has got your back- "Believe that!"

He may not come when you "want" Him "but" He's always on time! "Meaning."

God does not move on "wants' ' only on "needs' ' He already knows when to step in after you mess up, allowing sin to " fence" you in.

In a society, a world, "mad, mad, mad" I'm so happy, so ecstatic, so glad God has got my back!

All I need to do is talk, relate, allow Him to chart my destiny, rule my fate, "I" come away knowing He heard my humble cry, my feeble call... "stepped" right in removing sin's "sting" made everything 100% alright!

"Now, tell me" What man or woman can do that? "No one- absolutely no one! God proves time and time again "He's all that, and a bag of chips!" Without a doubt I know I must let go, I must let Him "work it out" instead of me acting on a

whim, “and” I must simply allow my weak faith to grow. “ Thank you, Lord,” for being “the Word” for saving grace to this hopeless dying human race!
“Selah”

Renea Simpson
12.13.14

Apostle Paul: Greatest Translator,
Salesman, Writer About Jesus' Ministry

While Jesus prepared His disciples to become "fishers of men", He looked down history's path to appoint a man who would take His (Jesus' gospel) further into history, throughout the world. Many years after Jesus' death, burial, and resurrections, such a man came on the scene.

Right Time, Right Place

Saul (later Paul) was bound for Damascus, Syria, on a mission for destruction, to persecute the Christians when Jesus Intervened. Jesus' intervention not only changed Paul 's life, it saved as well. Days after the intervention Jesus set Paul on a new job, an assignment to fulfill—praise God! Once converted Paul began his new mission preaching, teaching, converting heathens, to Christianity. Everywhere he traveled Paul gave very good sales pitches and arguments. By aid of the Holy Spirit, Paul's mouth was filled with the right words, affecting even the most "stone hearted" heathen to convert. Even King Agrippa was impressed by Paul, declaring, "Almost thou persuaded me to become a Christian (Acts 26:28)."
No Doubt

Comparing Peter to Paul is like comparing apples to oranges. As night is from day, Paul's gift to evangelize and speak was light years from Peter. Yes, Peter was given Hold Ghost power to preach, heal, convert sinners, yet his educational level was very minimal, in fact the Bible records Peter and the other disciples (with exception of Luke, a physician) as unlearned, simple fishermen.

Like his father, and generations before, all Peter knew was fishing, a trade he did for life. It is not surprising when Jesus called Peter, and the other disciples, He (Jesus), said, "I will make you fishers of men."

Paul's ability to speak thirteen different languages enabled him to spread the Gospel to places the disciples could not. He not only spoke to his salvation, but he also became a great ambassador for Christ!

What further set Paul apart from Jesus~ disciples were the fact the disciples were not just "unlearned", they wrote down the things Jesus did, the words He said, "as they happened," recording them for what is known as "The Gospels."

Paul, above all others, interpreted the meaning of those acts, deeds and helped come up with a cohesive Christian theology. In so doing, his courageous faith and preaching were important in the spread of the Gospel. Paul's writings and teaching were more influential than any Christian thinker, even to this day.

Humble Beginnings

At an early age Paul grew up in a well-to-do family of preachers and teachers, himself becoming a rabbi later in life. Paul had to learn a trade and so worked on the low paying hard task of tent making. Possibly during his teen years, he received teaching from skilled Jewish scholars, namely Gamaliel. His courageous, undaunted character caught the eye of Gamaliel when Paul was given the opportunity to study under the foremost teacher. As the saying goes, "the rest is history." God puts people in one's life at the right time, so it is no coincidence the gift for writing Paul learned under Gamaliel, God enabled him to write a greater part of the New Testament (eight epistles, total).

Paul wrote a greater part of the New Testament while a prisoner in Rome. These epistles (letters) are called "prison epistles".

Even though God had not given Paul the gift of an orator, I noticed Paul's one shining moment of public speaking recorded in Acts 13: 14-43. After entering the synagogue on the Sabbath day, Paul was invited to give words of

Here was God introducing Paul to the world. Once Paul stood, filled with the Holy Spirit, he delivered a powerful

speech, his words began with “Men of Israel, and ye that fear God, give audience”.

Side note: Shakespeare’s play, Julius Caesar, similar words were used, improvising the words of Paul in the scene where Cassius eulogizes Cassius eulogizes Caesar: “Friends, Romans, citizens, lend me your ears...we’ve come, not to honor Caesar, but to bury him...”

I am reminded of Martin Luther King giving his famous, powerful, soul stirring, “I Have a Dream” speech at the Lincoln Memorial steps, Washington, DC (August 28,1963). Both men of God left a “good” name, touching the world greatly.

Renea Simpson

12.15.14

Sunday Night Football

(Analogy of)

Dec. 29, 2013, at 8:35pm

While watching the Philadelphia Eagles (my favorite) play against the Dallas Cowboys, an analogy came to my mind: I pictured the game representing life's obstacles coming against the Christian.

Throughout the game there are first downs, second downs, third downs, fourth downs, tackles, penalties, offenses, (all not in that order), all repenting temptations and stumbling blocks in a Christian's walk. Once a touchdown is made it represents a Christian's victory, resistance against the wiles of the Devil.

Each fourth quarter of the game represents tests God puts Christian through. First test is the hardest because the Christian starts out a "babe" in Christ, Satan begins to throw every temptation and hindrance, many times, to cause the Christian to give up, possibly returning to his or her ways. But the pep talks of the team players to each other represent the Holy Spirit encouraging the Christian to persevere so he

she successfully makes it through each test, growing stronger in grace, while learning what all it takes to be a true follower of Christ.

As the game nears the end of the fourth quarter, it represents a Christian reaching his or her heavenly goal with Satan trying last futile efforts to destroy. The rising cheer of fans represents the heavenly host singing praise of salvation over you. Once the winning team makes that winning touchdown, it represents the Christian crossing over into everlasting life.

Renea Simpson

Inner Request

My mind, my soul, my heart... O Lord, strengthen these three and grant them a day's new start and lay upon each a reward of peace...

My heart, my mind, my soul... O Lord, thank you for love lighting upon my spirit like a dove as I grow old.

My soul, my heart, my mind... O lord, thank you for the power to forgive days people are not so kind! "Thanks" for reminding me that life is full of trouble, each day I live.

"Amen"

Renea Simpson
12.16.14

The 'Nation that Missed the Mark

Once a word history ago lived three masculine nouns, Destination, Rejuvenation and Procrastination. Each grew up well versed and affluently learned by nouns Pa and Ma Generation.

One bright beautiful autumn morning their nouns summoned them downstairs for special news. Each noun walked over to the couch, not sure if the news was good or bad. Once seated, each looking anxious, Pa Generation began his speech.

"Nouns, your Ma and I want to speak with you about your future". Pa Generation clutched his wife's hand lovingly before continuing. "Over these past twenty years we have watched you develop into fine articulate nouns never causing us worries. And over 80 these twenty years we too have been laying aside a nice inheritance for each of you. Today your mom I have discussed agreed to reward you with a percentage of your inheritance."

Taking notice their faces lighting happily Ma Generation added, "You are at that stage of taking responsibility, proving our labor was not in vain." "Therefore," Pa Generation interjected, "We are giving you ten percent for starters." " What's the stipulation?"

Practical thinking Rejuvenation questioned. Smiling proudly at his oldest noun's wisdom, Pa Generation answered candidly, "To prove responsibility, but most importantly, maturity. Question is- can you pass the test?"

His double round vowels traveled from one to the other. It was Destination who spoke up firmly "of course, we can pass the test, failure is not in our vocabulary." "That's right."

Rejuvenation added assuredly, "We will make you and Ma proud of us."

His double round vowels fastened upon Procrastination expectantly. "Yes, we will put our inheritance to good use. That's a promise."

Procrastination concluded softly.

"Outstanding! Nothing left to do now but disperse to you a ten percent portion." Each stood to their feet when Pa Generation fished out his wallet and approached them. Ma Generation wiped away tears of joy as she observed each noun hug their pa once he handed over a check.

"Thanks Pa, don't worry I'll do right with mine."

Destination whispered I, his ear. "Thanks Pa, I'll take all I' ve learned from you and Ma and be prosperous with mine".

Rejuvenation whispered in his ear.

"Thanks Pa, I already have big ideas on where this is going. I cannot wait to spend it". "Just make sure whatever you do is a good report". Pa Generation added sternly. He looked

suspiciously at his younger noun double round vowel check gleefully before stuffing it away in his pocket and walking away.

Rejuvenation came to his little noun's defense quickly.

"Don't worry Pa, I will make sure he does the right thing".

Pa Generation looked into his middle noun's double round vowels for a moment.

"One word history... that is what I am giving and expecting for a good report". With that he turned aside to the Ma Generation. Destination and Rejuvenation stood in silence and watched their nouns walk away toward the study.

Comparison Notes

How the masculine noun was spending their inheritance is clearly defined: eldest noun Destination blueprinted a New World dictionary housing 2000,000+ words. Elder noun Rejuvenation began breathing new life into old world words, spicing up a little slang along the way.

Yes, both invested their ten percent wisely whereas little noun run-on sentences his way through word history. Never once dotting his "I" nor crossing his "T" he preferred to recline on dotted lines. He continuously ridiculed his big nouns over how hard they were working.

"Man, you two work too hard. And for what? Don't you realize the three of us already have it made? Shoot! I say life is an easy road to travel, especially with a pocket full of

money and more stored up, just waiting for us".

Procrastination looked lazily over at his nouns. Sighing he replied matter of fact. "Live in the moment today...tomorrow is of no importance." "You are lazy, selfish, dangling participle," Destination scolded, "It is unwise of you to continue to preposition your way through word history. One day you are going to hit a big word block." "That's right," added Rejuvenation, "Ma and Pa expect you put your inheritance to good usage instead of run-on sentencing it and become a subordinate clause on Destination and me." " Aw stop with the judgmental adjectives! You two Wordsworth me more than a comma."

Procrastination argued defensively.

"C'mon little noun," Destination coaxed, "wouldn't you rather put your inheritance to good word usage? Picture your future tense—you will be among the first infinitive phrases of the Generation tree."

Destination prayed knowledge reached his little noun soon, for word history was passing quickly. But to his dismay Procrastination turned a deaf ear to wise words with a sarcastic reply. "No! Never! I would not like to waste my inheritance on no work. I intend to live my word history as one very incomplete sentence." Having said his intention, Procrastination walked away from his nouns for a final word history. "And so, behold our brother, Quadruple Negative."

Rejuvenation remarked sorrowfully. They continued looking after him sadly, knowing his word history would be one long endless run-on sentence.

The Journey

Over the course of word history vowels and consonants grew by leaps and bounds. Paragraphs tuned into pages...pages into chapter...chapters into a book. By a book' s end word history proposed well for Destination and Rejuvenation. All their hard verbs came to a harmonious definitive. Capitol began flowing into their word bank so fast until both partners incorporated their business thereby creating a hugely renowned dictionary still present to this day. Along the way Destination married a lovely little predicate adjective named Perky-Sweet. Together they made beautiful harmony. Happily, in love Destination had built a cute cozy

correlative conjunction spacious enough for the many little Destinations that would eventually be verbing around. Destination also appointed Perky-Sweet office manager. An aggressive appositive she made certain no misspelled, nor typos slipped by" accidentally. She definitely dotted every " I", crossed every "T"! Rejuvenation, the ultimate single noun, threw an elaborate wedding reception at his huge subordinate conjunction, inviting all their nouns and

pronouns. Good and bad, every relative was invited. They had the option of attending.

Destination casually strolled over to the table holding the list of relatives. Sitting down he scanned the list noting each checked name:

"Assignation, Bombilation, Carnation, Coronation, Culmination, Designation, Determination, Divination, Doctrinarian, Donation, Emanation, Examination, Explanation, Fascination, Illumination, Imagination, Impregnation, Incarnation, Inclination, Nomination, Ordination, Pollination, Predestination, Predetermination, Predomination, Ratiocination, Subordination, Abomination, Alienation, Alternation, Assassination, Consternation, Contamination, Damnation, Denomination, Deracination, Detonation, Discrimination, Disinclination, Disproportionation, Dissemination, Domination, Effemination, Elimination, Extermination, Fulmination, Glutination, Hallucination, Hibernation, Imagination, Incrimination, Indetermination, Indignation, Indiscrimination, Indoctrination, Insubordination, Peregrination, Procrastination, Recrimination, Resignation, Stagnation, Termination, Vaccination."

Checking out each noun and pronoun, Destination frowned.

"Say-why isn't 'Cras here?"

He was worried. Looking around the room, his double round vowels fell upon Rejuvenation conversing with his date. Walking Destination politely rested a hang on his shoulder.

"We have to talk." Rejuvenation turned around, a concerned look on his face. "Sure, Des'...excuse me babe."

Rejuvenation apologized to his date. He followed Destination to a spot they could talk privately.

"What's up Des'?" Rejuvenation asked concerned.

"Where is Procrastination? Didn't you send him an invitation?"

Silence. Rejuvenation laughed slightly.

"This is a great reception," Rejuvenation began, purposely diverting his double round vowels away from Destination " everything fell right into place". Only when Destination cast him a dark foreboding look did Rejuvenation start to tear up. "C'mon Des' -this is a joyous occasion- let's not ruin it with tragic news." "Tell me where he is now Juve." Destination pressed firmly. Rejuvenation signed long. He looked sadly at Destination.

Taking a stiff swallow of wine, he painstakingly broke the entire story down, from start to finish.

"Not too long after he received his inheritance 'Cras took off, moved to a big city called Ruination. His initial intention

was to buy a condo, place his money in a bank account, and live right for once..."

"Passing through the street near her corner; and he went the way to her house.

In the twilight, in the evening, in the black and dark night. And behold, there met a woman with the attire of a harlot, and subtle of heart..."

Rejuvenation paused, wiped away tears, cleared his threat and continued on. "That pipe dream went nowhere... 'Cras never even deposited a dime into any bank so it could draw interest. No, instead he began to gamble, started flashing, attracting trouble like a magnet. The first trouble he met was a sleaze named Destitution. Once she discovered his money "and " his weakness, she craftily, subtly ran a game on him big time. Man, in three months he had run-on sentences all his money, found himself broke and homeless. What little money he did have the sleazy fragment stole before she left him. ``

Destination, not really having the heart to, braved the question of Rejuvenation.

"So-where did he end up?" Rejuvenation shrugged my shoulders. "He's in prison Des'. Rejuvenation replied flatly.

"Prison?" Destination exclaimed disbelief.

"Yes, prison," Rejuvenation replied in a strangely calm voice. By now he had regained his composure. Both glanced around

to see if anyone had missed them. "But how-I mean- what did he do?"

Destination asked. "'Cras, as you know, was born to trouble. He never gave thought to the consequences of his actions. Anyway, he had to find the only other means of survival he could... which brought trouble for him again. He soon met up with three hoodlums named Would Have, Should Have and Could Have. Well, the word is 'Cras learned they planned to rob a word bank. Instead of breaking away from that tragedy he opted to go along. As you verbed correctly he and his partners in crime were arrested and hauled off to a prison called "Ruination". Destination shook his head sorrowfully. "I knew he would mess us... deep in my heart I knew he would".

"Like he said Des' ...live for today, tomorrow is of no importance".

"I had a bad feeling from the start he would mess up just like Pa did." Destination thought suddenly. His double round vowels looked into Rejuvenation.

"They don't know, Des' ...news hasn't reached home yet". Rejuvenation responded. "And now is not the time to tell them," Destination concluded wisely, "we must wait until later tonight when they can listen rationally". Unfortunately, there's nothing we can do for him now. All that's left for him now are incomplete sentences --- something he apparently

wanted". Both nouns shook their heads sadly. "We should be getting back to your reception. I'm sure everyone is missing us". Rejuvenation suggested. "Yeah, it's too late for tears anyway. I only pray he will be alright." Both hugged. Gathering their composure, they turned their attention back to the wedding reception.

<u>Moral of story:</u>
He becometh poor that dealeth with a slack hand: but the hand of the diligent maketh rich. He that gathereth in summer is as a wise son: but he that sleepeth in harvest is a son that causeth shame. Proverbs 10:4, 5.

Renea Simpson

Not So Soft Carpet

Randall's Inner Struggle

It is a fierce stormy Friday night, rain coming down in heavy sheets, wind howling like furocious wolves. Randall is struggling to focus, keep eyes peeled, and steady the car on the slippery streets, all along praying to make it home safely. Pulling up onto the driveway he breathed deeply, wiped away beads of sweat and shut off the engine. One inside his quiet dark apartment he went straight to his equally dark quiet bedroom, pitched keys upon the dresser and collapsed upon the king size bed. Turning over on his back he crossed arms on his chest and looked up at the white ceiling.

I ran from myself many, many times looking, not finding nowhere to hide "cost" of living reckless, "not willing" to accept sordid post "wouldn't" admit, time nor place sheltered security blanket "exposed" "forced" To turn, face sad sack in the mirror countenance holy terror! Soul living as walking dead not society's fault only me, myself I had to

dread "so" I pull self-pity off the shelf. "Couldn't" face dark cold evil I'd done, not asking forgiveness, not purging from consciousness, from rising to setting of Sun "hadn't" no one to blame "unable" to push pity party on anyone else "truly" I have to ride this train alone. On this cold dark Friday, I decided to end my life... What did I have to live for?? I have No kids, no wife, "so" riddled with guilt I sat on the right besides, reached into the drawer, quivering and pulling out a small pistol.

Face pensive, eyes tightly shut, I raised the side place to my left temple, sweat beads dancing my forehead, "while" mind forcing back dread index finger lingering on the trigger. Satan's voice, cold and steely, entered my head. "Go on, get it over with nigger, I've enjoyed turning your pathetic life from comedy to tragedy! Better for you, better for everyone you begin dead. "So" holding gun to temple Sweaty finger ready to squeeze, I accepted in another breeze I'd be gone. "Suddenly" trigger jammed "at same time" gun was "mysteriously" knocked out my hand no sooner hitting hard wood, jammed bullet escaped chamber "BANG!" Shattering scattered thoughts, striking a shoe in close range! Looking around, holding terror a calm strong male voice "replied" " Son, I had no choice... I did this for your own good. You chose to self-destruct- I intervened, struck the gun away. " Understand."

There's a better way to deal with issues, "talk to ME" I'll listen to all you have to say."

A gust of wind filled the room. I became overwhelmed at its mighty force overtaking me, knocking me upon each knee! At once deep remorse made me feel worse "yet" from somewhere I had a desire to be set "free." "Talk to me son" Strong voice repeated. Cupping hands over my face I wept bitterly, broken, defeated, "however" believing there was a better way "so" lying prostrate, I began to pray. "Lord" Listen... I'm no good with words, I might even ramble, "but "my life is a shamble, I pour my heart out to YOU... so much I've thought!

"Please help me." Right away persistent knocking upon the apartment door. Listing his face Randall set eyes upon the partially closed bedroom door. Listing himself off the not-so – soft carpeted floor he staggered out of the bedroom to answer the persistent knocker. *

Renea Simpson

The preverbal saying. *"An apple doesn't fall far from the tree " is certainly true. The proceeding writings are from my sweet niece, Tonya Elizabeth. I pray her written work touches your heart as it has certainly touched my heart.*
Renea Simpson

Disclaimer

Following Jesus is not easy, it involves not being fearful in the face of persecution, knowing Jesus does not leave you comfortless. He states, "Blessed are ye when men shall revile you, and persecute. you, and say all manner of evil against you falsely for my sake. Rejoice and be exceedingly glad, for great is your reward in heaven: for so persecuted the prophets which were before you." (Matthew 5:11,12).

I included Tonya's written works to be a blessing to single mothers like her. Yes, while there are closed-minded people ready to judge, it is a blessing to know *God is no respecter of persons (Romans 2:11).*

HE loves us in spite of our falling, HIS only request is to acknowledge Jesus Christ as our Lord and Savior, and t " get it right and tight" through Him before leaving this world. Once we seek His face, He brings us out of darkness into His marvelous light! As Jesus said to the woman caught in adultery, "Neither do I condemn you. Go and sin no more."

At the time of writing this book of poetry my niece was

single. By the time it goes into production she will be engaged, soon happily. married to a wonderful gentleman who loves her unconditionally. Through God all things are possible!

Renea Simpson

The Little Problem We Would Rather Ignore

By Tonya Elizabeth on Monday, August 27, 2012, at 4:15pm

Hi, I'm Tonya. I'm my mother's only child. I also have a child born out of wedlock. I have lied, gossiped and done many things in life that I'm not proud of. But still, in spite of this all, God loves me. I was rescued by the risen Savior and He has the power to save me from all things.

I opened this essay that way to get all the muck out the way. Transparent. Real and flawed. Even though the bible says there is no condemnation in Christ Jesus, we often condemn ourselves or live through perpetual condemnation in an institution where we should get the most help—The Church. This isn't me speaking poorly about my church or your church or any church in particular. It is a little note that suggests a little problem that many think about, but don't ever articulate. The Church is doing very little to save The World.

If the Church is defined as a group of people who believe in and worship God, then we can define The World as everyone else. The Church follows Christ. We are Christians. We

accepted Him and we are about The Great Commission.

We search for the lost and we celebrate when one person accepts Christ at church on Sunday.

But to follow someone means to walk the path they walk and to mimic their actions. A bit of observation about Jesus—He didn't really like The Church. He hung out with prostitutes, cheaters, liars and rebel rousers. He defended them when everyone thought they were guilty. He healed them when they seemingly deserved to die. He delivered them even though they were causing those around them problems. He had dinner with them even though the crowd couldn't see the significance of their lives.

That's right Jesus didn't care much for the INSTITUTION of the church. Those like the Sadducees and the Pharisees who studied and knew the word and worshiped God according to their traditions. The business of the church seemed to annoy him as He overthrew the tables and cast out the vendors from the front of the temple.

That's not us, right? We aren't spending our Sunday and Wednesday having worship services with each other. We are now looking for and receiving a "good Word" to further our agendas and purposes. Our book and worship CDs are to equip and discipline the Saints. We wouldn't dare do

this for the money, the fame or attention at the cost of presenting Christ to The World.
And now I go back to the problem. We, The Church, are falling to The World. We are trying so hard not to be of the World that we have no real interaction. We want people to know Jesus, but not at the cost of having our flaws show or business air. We are so far removed that we don't know the cry of their hearts. At our worst, we KNOW their heart's cry and turn our backs and ears from it.

It's more than a Merry Christmas. It's more than coming to visit us one Sunday. It's more than playing this cd to read this book. It's not the business of church that saves souls, it's the presentation of the risen Savior and letting The World see His work in your life.

The World may never come to your church, but they remember your cards and calls in their time of need. The World may never read Joyce Meyer or John Bevere, but they remember that you stopped by their desk to ask how their day was and cared. The World may never own an Israel CD, but they remember you asking how their mother was doing now that she's being cared for in hospice.

Be transparent. Care more. For once, allow your human side to be visible. Then, the true unfiltered God can shine through free from the filter of pretense and ready for Introduction to the World.

Learning and Living Life's Lessons

The older person who has inspired me most is my grandmother, Cora Simpson. Strong-willed and determined, she has never let any of life's obstacles deter her from her goals and dreams. Her witty nature and unstoppable stamina could easily place her as one of the most influential people in the twentieth century. Although she is not as well-known as Sandra Day O'Connor, Rosa Parks, or Oprah Winfrey, she still is influential to me. My grandmother's life has not only shown me that obstacles can be overcome, but dreams go on in spite of them.

My grandmother's life was never easy. Raised by her grandparents in the midst of the Great Depression, she always had to fight to keep her sanity and stay alive. She questioned herself daily about why her mother ran off and left her at the tender age of three. She was forced to drop out of high school and became a restaurant cook, supporting her grandparents, whose health was beginning to deteriorate. Taking care of her grandparents by day and working by night, she hardly ever had time to enjoy life like most of her friends. She married at age sixteen. Her marriage was not for love, but to better herself so that she could give her family the financial help that she could not

provide alone. She suffered the loss of her grandparents, husband, and eldest daughter all in a period of four years. Compelled by the realization that she needed to support her youngest child, my grandmother moved to Lima, Ohio, to help with the war effort in the 1940's. She returned to Florence in 1950 and remarried, a union that resulted in four additional children. Even though it appeared that she was happy, with the new marriage and newfound financial stability, the smile that she carried was a mere illusion. Not only was she having to work long hours to support the kids' schooling, but she was also facing the biggest battle that she had to fight before. She had become a battered wife. In spite of the stress that her husband put on her, Grandmother was still able to stay strong. Finally, she decided that no man could control her or her happiness, so she moved with the children into the home that she still lives in today.

Refusing to ever settle for less or even second- best, my grandmother accomplished most of her goals in life. Her career as a cook took her to several states across the Southeast and she even enjoyed a stint as a television cooking guru in the sixties. While she was unable to attend college or have everything that she desired, she provided a road to success for her children.

She saw three of them graduate from college and two enlist

in the military, traveling overseas. Her childhood friends never imagined that she would have so much happiness in spite of her troubles. But then again, never would my grandmother have either.

Tonya Simpson
March 14, 1998

An Undiminishing Light

Most of the things that I remember from my childhood happen during the summer. Sometimes I visualize them happening as dramatic movies, or even Broadway musicals, but mainly I view them as parables, each one teaching me a valuable lesson that would somehow help me later in life. Very early in my life, my grandmother devised a "You're supposed to learn this" list of things I should be familiar with as I grew older, but one of the most important values known to man apparently did not make it to her moral notebook pages. It was not until several years later that I was able to actually connect the valuable "lesson" of appreciating true beauty before it is too late with a childhood memory. I have learned that beautiful and pleasant things surround me daily. I will never know their true beauty or worth until after they are gone.

The most memorable part of my childhood was celebrating the Fourth of July with my family. Once the smoke cleared from the grill, and night blanketed the sky, we ended the festivities with fireworks. Though we had numerous missiles

and candles that elaborately painted the dark pallet above, none of the fireworks fascinated me more than the handheld sparklers. It was in these skinny metallic sticks that found the most delight.

Every year I raided the box like a bandit and wondered which part of the rainbow I held in my hands. Once lit, the sparklers radiated awesome hues of gold, silver and crimson. I would stand there and marvel at my "color stick," and ooh and ahh repeatedly like reciting a Gregorian chant. Then, suddenly, the spark stopped, its light a mere memory or enchanting dream.

Never did it occur to me that in front of my barbecue-stained face, I held an amazing wonder of science. It never seemed to matter that the colors were beautiful. Not once did I stop to notice its splendor. Just as I never took the time to appreciate the lighted sparkler, I did not realize how meaningful my LEAD experience was until after it was over. After months of anticipation and a long and bumpy flight, I had finally arrived at the campus. The scenery was breathtaking. Towering oaks and ethereal Gothic arches surrounded me. Feisty little squirrels played on the lush green

lawn, and each quad was furnished with wooden benches that were mainly used for meditation and staging. The scene embraced the soul of the beholder and encouraged the mind to be led by imagination.

I discovered many significant things during those long summer days in the hot Durham sun. While most of my days were spent in business classes, the most important knowledge I found I learned at the dorm from the rest of the people at camp. We all came from different backgrounds. We were economically, socially, regionally, and ethnically diverse. Though our words seemed so far apart, we did have a universal connection to each other. We are all smart. We each had something to share with one another about our lives. Most importantly, we were stuck in the Canterbury dorm together and somehow had to survive. To say the least, it proved to be the most amusing, terrifying, and interesting summer I have ever experienced.

Being the only person from Alabama, it was up to me to shatter the fictitious class of lies about the South that existed in the windows of their minds. "No, people do not turn around barefoot all the time. Yes, our schools have textbooks and

people can actually read. No, Mississippi Burning is not typical of race relations in the South and George Wallace is no tour symbol of democracy," I often found myself reciting in defense. The more I shared, the more eager they became to learn the truth. Similarly, I began throwing out stereotypes that I had about many of the other kids there. I learned that the kids at camp were just like me, with a few notable exceptions. We listened to the same music and read the same magazines. We wore many of the same clothing styles and had many of the same fears and dreams.

My roommate, Marie, proved to be the most helpful during my stay. I confided secrets in her that I had never told anyone else and for the matter never really admitted to myself. I saw a lot of myself in her and we were so much alike it was almost horrifying. It was almost as if my parents had lied to me all my life and never told me that I had a sister in Greenbrook, NC, but after evaluating the obvious discrepancies (Marie with Panamanian), I ruled out the theory. Every time that I had problems with classwork, with a guy, or with life in general, I seemed to mind. It appeared to make her happy to be a service to me, and it made me happy

to know she was there. Soon, the days grew shorter, and the hours passed by faster until both abruptly came to a premature end. Both Marie and my summer of Duke were gone and pages in a scrapbook of memories in my mind.

I lit a sparkler again this summer for the first time in about six years. I watched it radiate the same hues of gold, silver, and crimson, but a little more closely than before. While I anticipated the bursts of metallic rainbow, I was mainly prepared for the end. Internally, I praised its beauty. Internally, I sadly dreaded its end.

I have only talked to Marie once since I returned from camp. We shared stories of how our lives had changed since we returned home. I told her that I missed her more now than I did on those nights she camped out at the library. I told her how sad it made me that she was gone. There was something that I never could form the words in the mouth to say to her that day. No matter how hard I tried, I never was able to tell her that she was a beautiful person, or that deep inside, I would be better off if I were more like her. Somehow in the silent pauses on the phone, I guessed that she already knew.

A Firm Foundation

Although the wind blows fiercely in autumn and snow falls recklessly in winter, a storm tree survives. It does not falter because of the harsh conditions. Instead, the tree endures, and ultimately blossoms gloriously in spring.

Throughout my life, my family has taught me that in order to achieve my goals, I must have a keen sense of who I am and of what I believe. Also, I need to possess the ability to play whatever hand life deals me. I need a firm foundation. A value system that is composed of many elements will not only help mold me into a respectable person but will also propel me into becoming an even stronger individual in the future. Of these elements, there are two that influence me immensely. Remaining solid in my beliefs as well as being able to be bound back from life's setbacks, will help to encourage success at Baylor, and ultimately in life.

First Corinthians 16:58 says, *"Therefore, my believed brethren, be ye steadfast, unmovable, always abounding in the work of the Lord, forasmuch as ye know that your Labour is not in vain in the Lord."* This verse is the groundwork for much of what I believe. In high school, many things, particularly peer pressure, forced me to evaluate what I believed in and why I left these things superior to the pressures that I was under. If I decided to do drugs, skip

school, or cheat on tests, these things would only give momentary pleasure. If at Baylor or in life, as it was in high school, I face others who encourage me to do something that I do not personally endorse, I will stand up in the midst of mockery and ridicule and refuse to participate. An integral part of my value system is the notion that eternal pleasure comes in the long run. Yet, it only comes if I remain steadfast in my beliefs and continue doing what is right until the end.

Although many unfortunate things have happened to me, I have learned that the only way to succeed is to move on with my life. There may be a period of gloominess and desolation, but ultimately, happiness and hopefulness emerge. Coping with distressing mishaps, such as my mother's death and financial hardship, is an element of my value system that has been added as I go along. The most influential teacher I ever encouraged once told me, "When life serves you lemons, make lemonade." While one could make light of her words, I have jotted them down in the notebook pages of my memory for further references. Instead of sulking because these things have occurred, I find ways of coping. Though I cannot control what happens, dealing with problems as they come will prepare me for college or even the perils of the future. I know that success will result once I get up, dust myself off after

falling down. Success will result once I get up, dust myself off after falling down.

The fierce autumn wind and the harsh cold of winter easily uproot a weak tree causing it to waste away. Like a weak tree many who live blindly without a strong value system succumb to a life filled with bleak hopes and barren dreams. Instead, I feel that I am a strong tree. With my own value system firmly in place I will surpass my highest aspirations in college and in life. Thus, by being able to hold my ground in the times of temptation and trouble, I will succeed. Though the winds may blow strongly, and the cold winter will come I will endure until the end and blossom.

Tonya E. Simpson

October 17, 1997,

Last Minute Bits and Pieces

The Glass of Liquid

"The glass is half empty PESSIMISTIC or half full" it's optimistic how your third eye relates to look at it, per say. In the spiritual vision the glass is half full you're "intuit ably knowing" as you reach half level emptiness not to despair, God refills your glass assuring you, he has you, in his love and in his care.

Man, who looks at the glass as half full? Abraham when he answered his son Isaac:

"God will provide himself a lamb for a burnt offering." Genesis 22:8

Caleb silencing people when he gave a good report with from before Moses:

"We can overtake the land: Numbers 13:30, 14:19

Nehemiah proclaiming:

“Jerusalem can be rebuilt.” Nehemiah 2:16-20

David knowing God has got his back:
“Thou preparest a table before me, in the presence of my enemies: thou anointest my head with oil; my cap runneth over. Surely goodness and mercy shall follow me all the days of my life and I will dwell in the house of the lord forever. ” Psalm 23:5
Paul stated: *“We are more than conquerors.” Romans 8:37*
“Nothing will separate us from Christ.” Romans 8:38,39
Jesus stated the results of great faith (Mathew 21:21, 22). We should not look at the glass as half empty but half-full. God ALWAYS refills. This is another life lesson learned from the great Cora Elizabeth. God bless.

Renea Simpson

1.7. 2014

Meeting His Match

It is no coincidence that after His ascension back to Heaven, Jesus, so many years later, chose Paul to become one of His apostles. Jesus knew His first most outspoken apostle, Peter, would be killed, crucified upside down, so Jesus prepared another man with similar traits to Peter, with a few added incentives.

Peter the Rock

Peter was bold, courageous, defiant, and outspoken...Jesus therefore made him Leader, naming him "Petro" meaning "rock." But Peter's dark side was his rebellious hot temper, his inability to hold his tongue that made him speak without thinking, and his especially being arrogant and prejudiced. While Lord God does not want cowards in His army, He is displeased when a person lifts themselves up in pride, is arrogant and prejudiced. Of these sins God chastises with reproof and correction. There are two instances where Peter became prejudiced. Acts 2:28 where Jesus chastises him, and Galatians 2:11-14 where Paul chastises him. In both instances it was out of love.

Paul, the Man

Like Peter, Paul was also bold, courageous, defiant and outspoken. So-why was Paul, out of all the other apostles,

able to stand up to Peter and confront him? Scripture does not mention Peter being a bully but there are little innuendos one can detect. Impression is no one was brave enough to call Peter out when he sinned, yet Paul was not afraid of Peter. Look at Paul's character: he was a rebellious beast, a persecutor, so he quite possibly was more fierce than Peter. After Peter's encounter with Paul, Peter quite possibly developed a grudging respect for Paul, seeing him in a different light.

Message I took away from this is that sometimes the Lord God needs one of His sheep to correct another sheep when that sheep goes astray. Seniority does not matter...no one is above rebuke and reproof.

Renea Simpson
3.2.2015

A Case of Perpetrating a Front

Saturday night I accompanied friends to catch the movie, Get on Up (I consider the work put into bringing out the life and times of James Brown superbly done by Chadwick Boseman). The movie also focused on life lessons throughout.

One dramatic scene that intrigued me was the Famous Flames group calling a meeting and electing Maceo as spokesman or representative, to bring before James Brown their grievance of his (James) harsh treatments and willfully not paying everyone their salaries. This particular scene was similar to my pastor's sermon. In his sermon. In his sermon he spoke about Nicodemus being elected representative from his fellow Sanhedrin Counsel to seek out Jesus and ask him several questions. Going incognito, Nicodemus approached Jesus and tried the innocent game, "buttering" to Jesus with a weak compliment, but Jesus showed He was Master of the Game.

Jesus was so cool! I am handling every situation wisely, dissembling. John 2:24 shows how He knew all men... He knew what was in man. After answering Nicodemus' first question on man being born again with water and the Spirit, Nicodemus probed further with a second (in my opinion

"ignorant") question: "How can these things be?"
Jesus cut to the chase, directly asking Nicodemus, "Art thou a master of Israel, and knowest not these things?"
It is not surprising Nicodemus got snubbed... got played at his own game. He correctly remained silent, listening intently as Jesus dropped knowledge. No doubt Nicodemus became amazed at Jesus' knowledge, He was more advanced than Nicodemus and his fellow Sanhedrin. More importantly after his encounter with Jesus, he left a changed man, his life never being the same! Praise God!

Renea Simpson
8/4/2014

Do Right and Right Will Follow You

From childhood to teenage years, I often did "young and dumb" things, leaving my mother questioning my moral character, wondering if I were the same child she birthed into the world. "You're just climbing fool's hill" and "Do right, right will follow you" are two phrases she often spoke. Being inquisitive I pondered over her many wise words, wondering "Just what does she mean by that??" However, her phrase, "Do right, will follow you" intrigued me the most because for some reason it had a more effective power on my psyche.

More and more as I grew into adulthood, I experienced many sunny days and stormy days, traveled through many peaks and valleys and along the way I learned the meaning behind Mother's wise words. 113.

"Right" in the English dictionary means "following after what is just, good or proper; agreeing with a standard, facts or truth; what is appropriate, straight and genuine (real)." with a standard, facts or truth; what is appropriate, straight and genuine (real)."

Where is one place where all these adjectives are found except inside God's words, the Hold Bible, the ideal book of "realness."

Second Timothy states, "Study the bible to show thyself

approved unto God, a workman that needeth not to be ashamed, rightly dividing the word of truth." Diving deep into the Bible as it taught the ways of righteousness, I understood all the reading of the Word does one no good until action is made. So, to "do right" requires accepting Jesus Christ into your heart, into your life, taking up your cross and following Him. It requires practicing the "fruits" of the Spirit: love, joy, peace, long-suffering, gentleness, goodness, faith, meekness, temperance. (Galatians 5:22-23). Live in the Spirit as well as walk in the Spirit.

While it is important to not only be nurtured by your parents (Proverbs 22:6) it is very necessary to allow God to order your steps. Once you allow Him to order your steps "right will follow you." Yes, you will go through your sunny days and your stormy days, your peaks and valleys "but" with God in the midst you make it through.

I am appreciative of my mother imparting many wise words, and my taking time to listen and gain understanding. It is a lifelong gift I will cherish forever.

Renea Simpson

Not Just a Man's World

God knew a man could not survive without a woman,
God even said, "It is not good that man should be alone."
James Brown song "It's a Man's World" "But"
Even he knew the world would be nothing without a woman or a girl. Genesis 1:27 states, *"So God created man in His own image, in the image of God created he him; male and female created he them."*
God poured out His blessing upon a man and a woman giving them dominion over everything "so' it is very necessary on this men's and women's day for us to walk hand in hand, to work as a team within God's church. Once we do so our hopes and our dreams will manifest, the Church family will grow, Success will happen. Worship and Praise will become stronger "more importantly" Church life will flourish.
Once we give God our very best "so" Let's work together Let's stay together, "above all." Let's pattern our works after Matthew 6:33 going down on our knees, allowing God to nourish, when, to Him, we continue to pray Continue to obey.
Renea Simpson

It's All About the Cross

When He said, "It is finished" and
"Father, into Thine hands I commend my spirit."
Jesus became my savior.
Jesus became your savior.
Jesus became our savior.
That sixth to ninth hour
He was dying on Calvary.
The Cross
The Cross
It's all about the Cross.
Jesus paid ultimate price
For me
For you
For every single one of us
Peter's outright denial

Judas' callous betrayal
An innocent man
Enduring a mock trial
All in the name of LOVE
So, His FATHER would FORGIVE...
So, a way would be made to SAVE
Wretched sinners like us
The Cross
The Cross
It's all about the Cross Jesus paid ultimate price
For me
For you
For every single one of us

Today, Easter Sunday
We celebrate, rejoice
Our Savior conquering death
His resurrection on the third day
With all power and glory
"yes"
This story
Is the greatest story
Ever told Throughout history
The Cross

The Cross

It's all about the Cross

Jesus paid ultimate price

For me

For you

For every single one of us

"Amen"

Renea Simpson

The Man Who Thinks He Can

If you think you're beaten, you are;

if you think you dare not, you don't;
If you'd like to win, but think you can't
if almost a cinch you won't.
If you think you'll lose, you're lost,

for in the world, we find

success begins with a fellow's will;
it's all in the state of mind.

*

If you think you're outclassed, you are;
you've got to think high to rise.
You've got to be sure of yourself before
you can never win a prize.

Life's battles don't always go

to the stronger man;

But soon or late the man who wins

is the man who thinks he can?

Walt D. Wintle

In, Time

In life Nothing comes easy “thanks”
To Adam pain, misery, strife “became”
Big equation in our life. “thanks”
To Adam no one sails
Through life without fail
Even Job “proclaimed.”
Man, that is born of a woman is of
few days, and full of trouble.”

*

Time is “borrowed”
A debt we live on
Time is
A marathon runner
A sprinter
Pacing against history
Who, for better or worse,
Sings his/her swan song.
In place of doing nothing
Just practicing complacency,
Procrastination-Cy,” wasting”
A precious day, “begin”
Mornings with a prayer

“let” Your, mine, our
Time be valuable, “let”
Your, Mine, our
Heavenly Father knows
We appreciate
Second, minutes, hours
“given”
To celebrate
another day of living “out”
Of love “not” performing acts
Though a minstrel show.
Time waits
On no one
From rising to setting of the sun
A few hours are granted
To accomplish anything.

*

“So” Allow the Heavenly Father
To impart wisdom
To bestow guidance
To offer strength
While we travel
Life’s narrow way.

Renea Simpson

Incarnate Love

Love came down at Christmas,
Love, all lovely, love Divine;
Love was born at Christmas,
Star and angels gave the sign.

Worship we the Godhead,
love incarnate, Love Divine;
Worship we our Jesus:
But where is the sacred sign?

Love shall be our token,
Love be yours and Love be mine,
Love to God and man,
Love for plea and gift and sign.

Christina G. Rossetti

Bent Never Broken

Carrying his cross from mean streets of Jerusalem to
Golgotha Hill Jesus' body bent spirit never broken. "Yes"
Lord and savior Endured betrayal, cruel judgment, Beating,
flogging, mockery, spit, "yet" not a word had he spoken.
To Judas he directly replied, "What you must do, do it
quickly."
To Judas he sadly responded, "You betray your master with
a kiss?"
To the Sanhedrin Council he unapologetically answered, "I
and My Father are One."
To Pilate he unabashedly replied,
"You have no power over me."
To peter he truthfully said,
"Verily, verily I say unto you...before the cock crows thrice
you will deny me."
Out of his mouth Lord and Savior uttered.
Sweetest words ever spoken,
"Father forgives them for they know not what they do."
"then" with one final breath, with one last ounce of
strength, Lord and Savior uttered,
"Father, into thine hands I commend my spirit."
"Yes" on a rugged cross he hung dead with the bending of
his head "but" body was never broken.

Jesus is all about the greatest love of all.

John 15:1-17

Renea Simpson

After the Tears...the Hero Emerges

Year after year He fakes a front
He smiles outwardly
"fooling" "convincing"
"perpetrating"
Appealing every eye Yet
"dying" "crying"
Hating himself inwardly.
Year after year
He fakes a front
Convincing himself
All is lost...
His life has nothing left.
Year after year
He fakes a front
"Cowardly"
Curling into a ball upon narrow cold steel bed
Face against whitewashed wall "fighting"
Back angry tears
"realizing"
He wasted youthful years.
Year after year

He fakes a front
While hopelessly
Staring through one narrow window
To the outside world
Same world allowing him to be "robbed"
"enslaved" "shackled"
Precious freedom
"gone"
Now he sings prison songs
"wondering"
Why he gave privilege
For another man to
"entertain" His girl.
Year after year
He fakes a front
He is walking
"aimlessly"
Endless circles,
Within three cornered cells
"cold" "gray" "unfeeling"
Cesspool of hell.
Year after year
He fakes a front
He continually asks Himself,
"Where exactly, where Do I go from here?

Once I'm free---will anyone have love for me?
Should I bury wretched soul,
Always conform to this system
"and"
Continue to fake this front?"
Year after year
He fakes a front
He trudges onward
"unwillingly"
Enduring crazy mind games
Being called unflattering names
"yet"
He stays strong
Despite low points,
He focuses on high points,
"constantly"
Keeping sanity in check
"knowing"
Enduring this tragic wreck Would not last long.
After the tears
The hero emerges
"stronger" "resilient ""wiser"
He comes through "dark valleys"
He learns, After shed tears, After biggest fears,
"Survivors never give up."

When all else fails
God is there!
Call on HIM,
Lean on HIM,
Keep faith and trust in HIM! Through your storms,
HE will carry you!

Renea Simpson

A Classic Example Not Knowing How to Answer a Simple Open-End Question

One of many of our human flaws is hearing without listening. John 5:6-8 speaks of an experience between Jesus and crippled man. For thirty-eight years this man was unable to walk and perhaps for that same amount of time he was unable to dip himself into the pool of Bethesda when the angel troubled the water, healing other people.

Approaching him, knowing the cripple man's dilemma, Jesus asked him a simple one-end question, **"Wilt thou be made whole?"**

It was an easy question requiring little to no thought, only a direct answer (I.e., Matthew 9:28, 29 Mark 10:51/52) The cripple man took a trip all around the question. He was hearing, not listening. Perhaps he had become too overwhelmed, frustrated with his situation, he could not understand the Great Physician was standing before him, his time of being healed had finally come, requiring no dipping into the pool.

Understanding the man's "blindness" and inability to give a direct answer, Jesus had compassion on him. Instead of laying His healing hands upon the crippled man Jesus tested the crippled man's faith a second time, commanding

him to stand up, take up his bed and walk. From one verbal question to three commands requiring action, Jesus awaited a response from the man. This time the man " listened" ...he immediately, obediently did as Jesus commanded and had stepped out on faith this time.
My takeaway from this life lesson is Jesus knows our human frailties, but He leaves no room for excuses nor self-pity...we are obligated to show, not merely in words, but through action, our faith and belief in Him. Our faith should not be small but as big as a mountain, which we should also believe we can move.

Renea Simpson
3/2/2014

Blessed Imperfection

And the Lord God caused a deep sleep to fall upon Adam, and he slept: and He took one of his ribs and closed up the flesh thereof: and the rib, which the Lord God had taken from man, made. He was a woman and brought her unto the man. And Adam said, "This is now bone of my bones, and flesh of my flesh: she shall be called Woman because she was taken out of Man. Genesis 2:21-23

First open chest surgery as administered by God, a procedure conducted out of love and necessity. By necessity all the creatures God created, and Adam named had the luxury of mating with their kind. Adam needed someone in his likeness he could relate to, by love someone he could relate with. someone compatible with him. As God stated to His Son, *"It is not good that the Man should be alone: I will make him help me meet him. Genesis 2:18*

Hence the creation of Woman
A recent survey stated there are ninety-four million Mothers in the United States. On Sunday, May 11th, 2014, ninety-four million mothers will wake up and experience the day bestowed by expressions of love. Ninety-four million mothers will cry tears of happiness that gain, another year,

she is celebrated. All mothers are born a woman. Like my mom, all mothers have faults and shortcomings, "yet" mothers possessing that same virtuous characteristic as my mom had possessed, are richly blessed by God. Like Mother Eve who was perfect in the beginning before falling to sin, and made imperfect, mothers are creatures of blessed imperfection by God.

The American Heritage dictionary defines virtuous as " exhibiting virtue; possessing or characterized by virtuous women" is found in Proverbs 31:10-31. Solomon stresses how much praise is given a virtuous woman. Twelve times she is in action, doing a worthy cause for her family, her community, herself. Her husband is shown a happy man blessed to have a good woman. *A virtuous woman is a crown to her husband but she that maketh ashamed is as the rottenness of his bones.... Proverbs 12:4).* By his side and his chastity; pure: a virtuous woman." The portrait of a side and he is highly respected in his community. Last of all, in verses thirty-one and thirty-two, Solomon speaks of a virtuous woman given her just reward, the Lord even giving her much praise!

Last of all, in verses thirty-one and thirty- two, Solomon speaks of a virtuous woman given her just reward, the Lord even giving her much praise! So, to all mothers everywhere-

-- Happy Mother's Day! Make your day filled with adoration, celebration and spiritual praise to God!

Renea Simpson

Rising Above the Fracas and the Rubble

"Wear the world as loose garment." "Take Jesus to be your friend."

Words my mother spoke...I understand their meaning as I become older and wiser more and more each day. In these last days people have become worse cynics and hypocrites, it is necessary to stay rooted and grounded in God's Word, focus totally on Him in everything we say, do or think--- " Order my Steps in Your Word" as the song states.

When we move and have our being through God, He gives us power to fight against any obstacle that comes against

us, so we rise above fracas and rubble. In dealing with negative people, Matthew 5:11,12 are verses I live by.

"Blessed are ye, when men shall revile you, and persecute you, and shall say all manner of evil against you falsely, for my sake. Rejoice, and be exceedingly glad: for great is your reward in heaven, for so persecuted the prophets which were before you."

Renea Simpson
3.2. 2014

House United Love Undivided

(Years of space)

A house is a structure serving as a dwelling place for one or several families, a place of residence.)

So- what holds or keeps the structure together? First, living by faith...second walking in the Spirit. Faith comes alive when work is involved. This work requires focus, order and teamwork. Focusing on God the Father. God the Son, one's blueprint of constructing a house is of order not chaos and being on one accord makes teamwork. James 2:14-26 illustrates faith that works and Hebrews 11 (the faith chapter) defines faith, giving examples of soldiers who stepped out of faith and lived by faith.

Then there is walking the Spirit. How one walks in the spirit is to walk in the newness of life (Romans 6:4) and not after the flesh (Romans 8:14), also remembering to walk by faith not by sight (2 Corinthians 5:7). Paul states *" Therefore if any man be in Christ, he is a new creature: old things have passed away; behold, all things have become new." (2 Corinthians 5:17).* So- what keeps a house united, love undivided? Not meekness, temperance against such there is no law (judgment) Galatians 5:22, 23. When these steps are followed a house becomes home.

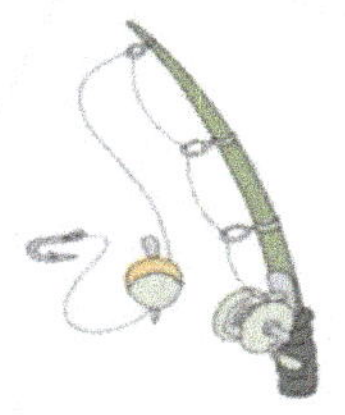

Gone Fishing

December 28, 2013, at 8:25 am

The Devil goes fishing with cleverly designed fishing pole and *spiked* bait to catch fish.
BUT GUESS WHAT?
Jesus goes fishing WITHOUT neither fishing pole nor bait AND STILL catches fish!
PRAISE GOD!!!!

Renea Simpson
12.13.14

Satan was stripped of his talent to sing, lead the Heavenly choir, when he lost his mind thinking he could be like God, maybe higher than HIM. It goes to show pride goeth before a fall, fall meaning a person placing his/herself outside of God's realm.

God's Promise

Although things are not perfect
Because of trial or pain
Continue in thanksgiving
Do not begin to blame
Even when the times are hard
Fierce winds are bound to blow
God is forever able
Hold on to what you know
Imagine life without His love
Joy would cease to be
Keep thanking Him for all the things
Love imparts to thee
Move out of Camp Complaining...
No weapon that is known
On earth can yield the power
Praise can do alone
Quit looking at the future
Redeem the time at hand
Start every day with worship
To "thank" is command

Until we see Him coming

Victorious in the sky

We'll run the race with gratitude.

Xalting God most high

Yes, there'll be good times and yes some will be bad,

but....

Zion waits in glory... where none is ever sad!

Same Message Different Wording

(An idle mind & laziness)

A mind is a terrible thing to waste. ---United Negro College Fund An idle mind is the Devil's workshop.

And withal they learn to be idle, wandering about from house to house, and not only idle, but tattlers also and busy bodies, speaking things which they ought not. ---1 Timothy 6:13

Slothfulness casteth into deep sleep; and an idle soul shall suffer hunger. --Proverbs 19:15

The slothful man sayeth, "There is a lion in the way, a lion is in the streets." As the door turneth upon his hinges, so doth the slothful upon his bed. The slothful hideth his hand in his bosom; it grieveth him to bring it again to his mouth.

The sluggard is wiser in his conceit than seven men that can render a reason. ---Proverbs 26:13-16

For even when we were with you, we commanded you, that if any would not work, neither should he eat. ---2 Thessalonians 3:10

Did you know?

Research indicates that people who laugh a lot are much healthier and may live longer than those who don't find time to chuckle. A good, deep laugh can provide your body and mind with a great workout. Dr. Lee Burk at the Loma Linda School of Public Health in California found that laughing lowers levels of stress hormones and strengthens the immune system. The organization ***Laughter Works,*** which teaches people how and why to laugh, says laughter can cause blood pressure to drop, blood to become oxygenated and endorphins to kick in, which can improve mood. And that's just the beginning. Laughing can help reduce stress and promote stronger relationships between people who laugh together. Data indicates children around the age of six laugh the most, laughing roughly 300 times per day, while adults average only 15 to 100 laughs per day.

From me to You

Most people don't realize spiritual truth as "love in action." Simpsonly the Best Spiritual Truths are my written works of love in action from my perspective.

As God's Word, the Bible is love in action, so is everyday living. From morning, when our eyes open, until nighttime when we retire to bed and close our eyes for sleep, we are accountable for all the hours in between. So, the question is in those hours did our action and our words sow love, or did they sow hate? At the end of the day only we can give an honest analysis of ourselves, for all is accounted for by God.

My belief in life is expressed this way:

Meeting mornings with a smile
Sitting, reflecting for a while,
Appreciating God giving your life
As a mother gives birth to her child.

*

Never dwelling on past mistakes
Seizing opportunities before it is too late;
Realizing life is not a game
It is a serious business
Once gone, fortune and fame

All that is left of your memories
Hopefully a good name.

*

Monies are accumulated blessings
From God's bank!
Take a moment to give HIM thanks
Make timely deposits
To reap an abundant withdrawal!

www.ingramcontent.com/pod-product-compliance
Lightning Source LLC
Chambersburg PA
CBHW071944190726
48293CB00004B/1331

* 9 7 8 1 9 5 6 8 8 4 1 5 9 *